CU00847013

A GAY FLASH BACK

"We should indeed keep calm in the face of difference, and live our lives in a state of inclusion and wonder at the diversity of humanity."—George Takei

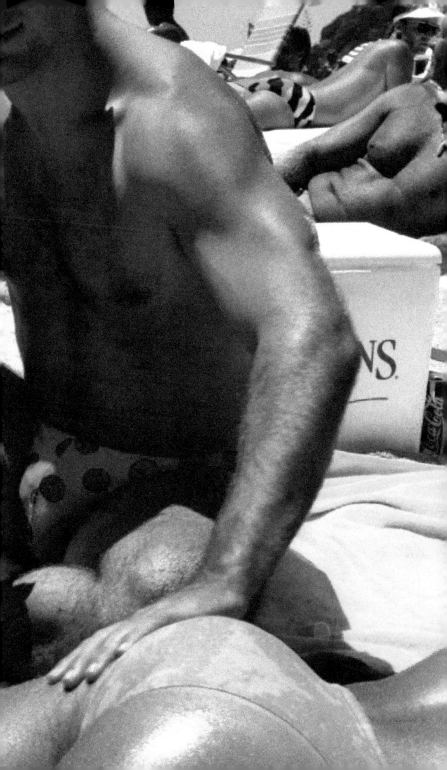

CPSIA information can be obtained
at www.ICGtesting.com
Printed in the USA
BVHW021638300719
554670BV00011B/209/P